T0208898

# A WORKING FELLOWSHIP WITH JESUS, YOUR LORD

## THE FRUIT OF THE SPIRIT BIBLICAL STUDY

## CARLTON BAKER

WESTBOW
P R E S S*
A DIVISION OF THOMAS NELSON
& ZONDERVAN

WestBow Press books may be ordered through booksellers or by contacting:

WestBow Press
A Division of Thomas Nelson & Zondervan
1663 Liberty Drive
Bloomington, IN 47403
www.westbowpress.com
1 (866) 928-1240

Because of the dynamic nature of the Internet, any web addresses or
links contained in this book may have changed since publication and
may no longer be valid. The views expressed in this work are solely those
of the author and do not necessarily reflect the views of the publisher,
and the publisher hereby disclaims any responsibility for them.

Any people depicted in stock imagery provided by Getty Images are
models, and such images are being used for illustrative purposes only.
Certain stock imagery © Getty Images.

Unless otherwise indicated, all Scripture quotations are taken from the Holy
Bible, New Living Translation, copyright © 1996, 2004, 2015 by Tyndale House
Foundation. Used by permission of Tyndale House Publishers, a Division of
Tyndale House Ministries, Carol Stream, Illinois 60188. All rights reserved.

Scripture quotations marked (NIV) are taken from the Holy Bible, New
International Version®, NIV®. Copyright © 1973, 1978, 1984, 2011 by Biblica,
Inc.™ Used by permission of Zondervan. All rights reserved worldwide. www.
zondervan.com The "NIV" and "New International Version" are trademarks
registered in the United States Patent and Trademark Office by Biblica, Inc.™

ISBN: 978-1-9736-8494-7 (sc)
ISBN: 978-1-9736-8493-0 (hc)
ISBN: 978-1-9736-8495-4 (e)

Library of Congress Control Number: 2020902023

Print information available on the last page.

WestBow Press rev. date: 02/05/2020

# CONTENTS

This book has its roots in years of study seeking answers to many questions. Specifically my goal was to understand precisely what Paul meant when he said: It's the fruit of the Spirit and not fruits of the Spirit. I was faced with many questions including: "What then is the fruit of the Spirit?" And "How does the manifestation of this fruit take shape in our life?" As I discovered the meaning and relevance of this short passage of Scripture I learned and experienced what I call liberation from the usual easy answers and from the pressure to perform according to traditional rules and perceptions. As I grew in understanding I also matured in rejoicing in the liberty of doing what Jesus desires of me. I joyfully understood I was not alone. I was set free from the depressing and frustrating experiences of depending upon my own strength, skill and wisdom. Incredibly I learned that Jesus said He and I were partners in ministry. This is His incredible design and not my theological predisposition. In light of this new working relationship with Jesus I moved forward with liberating joy and honest expectation. The phrase "You love them and I will change them" took on new meaning. I encourage you to read this book with an open heart. I believe you too will discover a new freedom and joy in being a follower of Jesus.

The following is an important note to be read. It is a key to understanding your role in living life in the fruit of the Spirit.

A working fellowship with Jesus, your Lord. John 15:1–17 (My notes added in brackets.)

Listen to Jesus.

I am the true vine, and my Father is the gardener. He cuts off every branch that doesn't produce fruit, and he prunes the branches that do bear fruit so they will produce even more. You have already been pruned for greater fruitfulness by the message I have given you. Remain in me, and I will remain in you. [Why? Jesus explains.] For a branch cannot produce fruit if it is severed from the vine, and you cannot be fruitful apart from me. [This is a working fellowship with Jesus.] Yes, I am the vine; you are the branches. [We are significant.] Those who remain [abide] in me, and I in them will produce much fruit. For apart from me you can do nothing. [We are not to go it alone.] Anyone who parts from me is thrown away like a useless branch and withers. Such branches are gathered into a pile to be burned. But if you stay joined [abide] to me and my words remain in you, you may ask any request you like [in prayer], and it will be granted! My true disciples produce much fruit. [We can live with godly expectations.] This brings great glory to my Father. I have loved you even as the Father has loved me. [Do you really believe this incredible truth?] Remain in my love. When you obey me, [the mandate] you remain in my love, just as I obey my Father and remain in his love [the model]. I have told you this so that you will be filled with my joy [the promise]. Yes, your joy will overflow! I command you to love each other [the mandate repeated] in the same way that I love you [the model once again]. And here is how to measure it—the greatest love is shown when people lay down their lives for their friends. [It's not just talk.] You are my friends if you obey me. I no longer call you servants, because a master doesn't confide in his servants. Now you are my friends, since I have told you everything the Father told me. You didn't choose me. I chose you. I appointed you to go and produce fruit that will last [the working fellowship] so that the father will give you whatever you ask for, using my name. I command you to love each other. [Love is the key.]

## Listen to Paul.

Paul assures us: "But we have this treasure in jars of clay to show that this all-surpassing power is from God and not from us" (2 Cor. 4:7, NIV).

## Listen to History.

History confirms this truth: Commentators both ancient and modern agree that love is the root of all of the fruits in Gal. 5:22–23; in fact, they are manifestations of love—the chief Christian virtue, the one that will last forever (1 Cor. 13:8). The church father Jerome remarks, "Without love other virtues are not reckoned to be virtues. From love is born all that is good" (ACCNT vol. 8, p. 85). God is love (1 John 4:8), and to imitate Him as we walk by the Spirit is to love others" (TABLETALK, April 2009, p.29).

<u>Listen to "Self."</u>

What are your expectations when you ask for any of the manifestations of love? Too often, we ask for a "spiritual pill." That is, we are involved in a situation and we pray for patience or self-control or a manifestation of love. The result is that nothing happens, and then we wonder why! We don't need a "spiritual pill"; we need the love of God to control our hearts and minds and tongues. This idea will be emphasized throughout this book. It is God's love that manifests itself in joy, peace, patience, and more.

I know when I become impatient it is because I have focused on myself and not on the love God has given me. It has become about self-control rather than trust in him who loves me and who has gifted me to live in his love. So, an important factor is to listen to *self.* What is *self?* Expecting and expressing and wanting things apart from the love of Jesus. Remember that you have been gifted with a working fellowship with Jesus. Rejoice in it. Trust him. Relax and live in his love. Know that he can do exceedingly above all that you ask or can even imagine.

<u>Celebrate your partnership.</u>

Celebrate in freedom, knowing that you are not called only to do what Jesus can do; you are doing what he has called you to do. Celebrated with honest expectation because you know he is capable and will do what he says he will.

# Assemble as Designed

My experience as a machine designer

The gentleman stopped at my desk and asked, "How do I assemble all those parts that have been placed on my desk?" He was experienced in assembling machines; however, the parts he spoke of were for a new machine he had never assembled before. His question was legitimate. He came to me because I was the one who had designed it. I understood the purpose of this machine and how it was to be properly assembled.

I visited with him at his workbench. Sure enough, there was a variety of odd parts spread across his workbench. No wonder he was perplexed. I first explained the purpose of the machine—about how it was to function and what it was designed to produce. Then, looking at the blueprints and each of the parts, I explained how it should be put together. He accomplished the task expertly. The result was a machine that was properly assembled and that functioned as designed.

Here's the question: What do you think the result would

have been if he had decided he knew better than the designer? Suppose he thought he could make it better by doing it his way. What do you think the result would have been if he had assembled it according to his own concept?

Just like this assembly man, every day, we have the choice to assemble our life according to our maker's design or according to our own desires. The results are obvious and tragic. Adam and Eve chose to live according to their own desires rather than by the clear instructions from their maker. They believed they could do it better. That was their rebellion against God, resulting in a tragedy that still affects us today. This principle lays the foundation for understanding what God meant when he counseled us to live by the fruit of the Spirit. It is self-evident that living by the fruit of the Spirit is the key to a God-centered life as opposed to living by the desires and expectations of our sinful nature (Gal. 5:16–26).

# THE IMPORTANT QUESTION

God's desire for his people is for them to live according to his design. This raises a very significant question: What did Paul mean by "the fruit of the Spirit"? How we understand this statement manifests in how we respond to the daily issues of life. For years, I asked myself many questions, seeking to better understand what the Bible taught about the fruit of the Spirit. For instance, why did Paul say fruit of the Spirit and not *fruits*? Why did translators change *fruit* to *fruits*? Perhaps it was because Paul listed nine fruits, and therefore, the singular *fruit* was changed to the plural *fruits*, and *is* was changed to *are*.

That did not make sense to me—especially because the Greek is clear: "the "fruit of the Spirit is" *not* "the fruits of the Spirit are." From my searching of the scripture, I concluded that we are to understand that Paul, under the guidance of the Holy Spirit, stated exactly what he was guided to say. This meant that I was to understand it just as Paul meant it to be understood. How could I get ahold of this fruit and incorporate it in my life? Was it mystical? Did I have to pray and wait for a special blessing? How practical was it? What could or should I do to experience these qualities of love in my life? What did God expect of me? And so the questions went, eventually leading to a biblical study of the fruit of the Spirit. It became challenging, life-enriching, and life-changing.

Striving to put these nuggets of truth into practice continues to be a daily experience. Sometimes I succeed and rejoice. Many times, I fail miserably—but even that becomes a learning experience. It was and continues to be a matter of growth. This study reflects my many years as a husband, a father, and a pastor. As a student of God's word, I always strive to understand and teach the practical dimensions of the Christian faith. Equally true, I want the spiritual fruit to be evident in my life. This study material is an effort to share with others that which I have learned and continue to experience.

# God's Love Is the Key to Understanding

In my searching, I recalled what Paul said about the gift of love. "Hope does not disappoint us, because God has poured out his love into our hearts by the Holy Spirit, whom he has given us" (Rom. 5:5, NIV). He has poured his love into us. That's incredible! Therefore, my initial conclusion was that the fruit of the Spirit is love. This love is to produce evidence, qualities, of this gift that God has poured into me. It is significant to note the context of this gift. Notice how God describes you and me. This is who we are in his eyes. We were powerless (6), ungodly (6), sinners (8), and his enemies (10). Wow! It is hard to believe that such a treasure would be poured into such unworthy, broken vessels, but God knew what he was doing.

<u>Jesus questioned by a lawyer</u>. One of them, an expert in religious law, tried to trap him with this question: Teacher, which is the most important commandment in the law of Moses? Jesus answered with just fifty words, "You must love

the Lord your God with all your heart, all your soul, and all your mind. This is the first and greatest commandment. A second is equally important: Love your neighbor as yourself. All the other commandments and all the demands of the prophets are based on these two commandments" (Matt. 22:35–40). It becomes self-evident that love is the key.

<u>Jesus's command to his disciples.</u> Near the end of Jesus's earthly ministry, he gave his disciples a command and model to practice. "So now I am giving you a new commandment: Love each other. Just as I have loved you, you should love each other. Your love for one another will prove to the world that you are my disciples" (John 13:34–35). Again, love is the key.

With utter amazement and joyous expectation, we can read how Paul describes this gift that God has poured into every believer. We are broken vessels in constant need of God's grace, enabling us to live in such a manner. What follows is 1 Cor. 13:1–7, from the New Living Translation. This is a long quote, but you will be enriched by reading it carefully and thoughtfully.

> If could speak in any language in heaven or on earth but didn't love others, I would only be making meaningless noise like a loud gong or a clanging cymbal. If I had the gift of prophecy, and if I knew all the mysteries of the future

and knew everything about everything, but didn't love others what good would I be? And if I had the gift of faith so that I could speak to a mountain and make it move, without love I would be no good to anybody. If I gave everything I have to the poor and even sacrificed my body, I could boast about it; but if I didn't love others, I would be of no value whatsoever. Love is patient and kind. Love is not jealous or boastful or proud or rude. Love does not demand its own way. Love is not irritable, and it keeps no record of when it has been wronged. It is never glad about injustice but rejoices whenever the truth wins out. Love never gives up, never loses faith, is always hopeful, and endures through every circumstance.

**The Principle.** In living the God-given command to love as he loves us, it is important to remember that we love because God first loved us. That is our motivation. It is our driving force. It is our purpose. Anything else comes from self-centeredness. To love someone in order to change them is not an example of God-love, but rather, another form of self-centeredness. God's love does not seek to manipulate others. It is not done for self-gratification. It does not seek to control us. Be alert in practicing God's love so that it does not become a tool for manipulation, legalism, or self-aggrandizement.

God-love is God's command to, and desire for, his people to extend His grace into everyday situations and relationships. In doing so, it is crucial to remember that it is only when God pours his life (*zoe*, in Greek) into a person that he or she will come alive in Christ (Rom. 8:5–8). The astonishing truth is that God, in his mercy, love, and wisdom, has called his people to be instruments of his grace by extending his love into everyday situations.

Now, let's see how we can experience these expressions of God's love: joy, peace, patience, kindness, goodness, faithfulness, gentleness, and self-control.

# JOY:
# A MANIFESTATION
# OF GOD'S LOVE

I remember being in a small group years ago. We spent considerable time discussing what was meant by *joy*—and, particularly, how it is distinguished from "happiness."

Author Phillip Keller puts it into a clear perspective. In his book *A Gardner Looks at the Fruits of the Spirit*, he writes:

> Joy and happiness are not the same ... Each springs from a totally different source. One comes from the world around me. The other originates directly with the Spirit of the Living God. Happiness is conditioned by and often dependent upon what is "happening" to me. It is irrevocably bound up either with the behavior of other people, the sequence of events in my life, or the circumstances in which I find myself. If these are going well in

one way or another I am said to be "happy." If, on the other hand, my circumstances are adverse I am described as "unhappy." Joy, on the other hand … throbs throughout the Scriptures as a profound, compelling quality of life that surmounts and transcends the events and disasters which may dog God's people. Joy is a divine dimension of living not shackled by circumstances.

Here's a question to ask yourself: What happens to joy when we become critical of others or angry or negative? We can't enjoy others for what—or who—they are. We fail to enjoy life around us. We may even lose a good night's sleep. We can't enjoy a delicious meal or enjoy our mates. We feel imprisoned. Life becomes a very small circle that includes only ourselves and our feelings. We are trapped!

Jesus tells us that we are to remain in his love and therefore experience his joy. He is communicating truth to us so that *his* joy will be in us and *our* joy will be complete. Now, that is an extraordinary statement! In fact, it is so astounding that we have trouble grasping it. Almost immediately, our minds question the possibility of such an amazing statement (John 15:9–12).

Joy is the result of believing in and being what God

wants us to be. It means living the way God desires. This is God-love in action, and the result is joy that transcends the circumstances of our lives. Every day, we are challenged in a variety of ways, and we easily become trapped. Consider a few everyday traps that rob us of joy.

## The Trap Called *Circumstances*

We usually have no control over our circumstances. We are involved whether we like it or not. The disciples Paul and Silas had a very successful ministry, but then the religious and political leaders turned against them (Acts 13:48–52). Even the crowds joined in the attack. They were stripped and severely flogged. Remember, no Roman citizen was to be treated this way without a trial (Acts 16:37). Talk about injustice! But that is not all.

They were then thrown into prison, into an inner cell, with their feet fastened in stocks. Wow! Within a short period of time, their lives had been painfully disrupted—turned upside down. Can you imagine the pain from being severely flogged? Can you imagine the discomfort of having your feet locked in stocks? Can you imagine faithfully serving the Lord and then, seemingly, all of life turns against you? About midnight, Paul and Silas were praying and singing hymns to God (Acts 16:22–25).

Honestly, how do you think you would respond? Would

it not be natural to ask, "Why, Lord? How could you let this happen? If you are sovereign and loving, why is this happening?" Would you respond with singing? Our natural responses to trials are anger, frustration, bitterness, envy, negative thoughts, retaliation, and other such attitudes that flow from our sinful human nature. The question before us is this: What enabled Paul and Silas to be filled with such joy that erupted in praise?

It could only be that their hearts and minds were filled with the assurance of God-love. It is this reality that caused such a response. Their attitudes resulted in a joy that led to singing. Even such severe circumstances could not rob them of this joy, rooted in God's love despite the circumstances.

The truth is, God has poured his love into every believer by the Holy Spirit (Rom. 5:5). Is this not an encouragement and exhortation to respond to life out of this gift that God has put in us, rather than responding from our own strength and self-centeredness? It requires belief and confidence in God.

Joy is an attitude we develop as a result of living in coherence with the Holy Spirit that is in us. This is what enables us *not* to succumb to our circumstances. Joy is the result of not letting the circumstances control us, but rather drawing upon the resource of God-love to control us. When we live as God desires, we will experience his joy in our lives, rising above our circumstances.

## The Trap Called *People*

People can be a meaningful source of joy but also a source of frustration. They can rob us of joy if we let them. The fact is, we easily become trapped!

A pastor was imprisoned during the Nazi reign of terror. He related how he experienced severe deprivation of basic human dignity. He lived in the worst situation conceivable. He was not treated as a person. He was just a number. He experienced incomprehensible hatred. He was trapped! But incredibly, he did not let the hatred of his captors destroy him. How was he able to survive? "I am not one of them," he said. "I belong to Jesus." In this place, filled with the hatred of his captors, he ministered the love of Jesus to his fellow prisoners. God-love was in control of his mind, attitude, and actions.

Christ is your example (1 Pet. 2:21). The Greek word for example, *hupo/grammos*, means under/write. Remember the early years in school when you practiced your penmanship? You wrote underneath a perfect example—or, at least, you tried. In the same sense, Jesus is our perfect example and we are to follow in his steps. Think about it. Since Jesus is our *hupo/grammos*, what is God's desire for us? Imagine standing at the foot of the cross. It is there you see the love of God (the vertical dimension of love) that was motivating Jesus to die (the horizontal dimension of love) for you. Continue reading verses 21–25 for this principle. Think about how this applies to your life.

> Follow in his steps. He never sinned, and he never deceived anyone. He did not retaliate when he was insulted. When he suffered, he did not threaten to get even. He left his case in the hands of God, who always judges fairly. He personally carried away our sins in his own body on the cross so we can be dead to sin and live for what is right. You have been healed by his wounds! Once you were wandering like lost sheep. But now you have turned to your Shepherd the Guardian of your souls. (1 Pet. 2:21–25)

What has Jesus done for you and me? How are we meant to live according to these verses? Again, it is the love of God that controls our sinful nature. We are to respond to life in the gift of love that he has planted in us. Obviously, it takes more than our human strength to respond in this way, but we have been healed. We have a shepherd. We are equipped to respond supernaturally. This means that we should have trust and confidence in Jesus, our Lord. It means we should nurture this quality of love in our lives and practice it daily. At this stage in our lives and in our working relationships with Jesus, it is not perfection he expects, but rather, a godly attitude and growth.

People can rob us of joy but can also be a source of great joy. This is particularly true for believers. We are also meant to be a source of joy to others. No wonder Jesus commands us to love one another as he loves us! Even our words are meant to be a source of joy to others. Our words should be used to build others up, not criticize and tear them down. They should be helpful and beneficial, as noted in Eph. 4:29. Again, this is the principle. When our hearts and minds are filled with God's love, we will respond how Jesus has empowered us to. If not, we will respond out of our self-centeredness. When you find yourself in a situation, ask what the basis of your wordsare. That is—why did you respond as you did? Did you express yourself out of God's gift of love? Were you conscious of your working fellowship with Jesus, your Lord?

## The Trap Called *Things*

Being possessed by things can quickly rob us of joy. Everything, except God, is subject to change or fluctuation, fads, and fashion. Everything in this world undergoes decay and devaluation. Yet, despite the transitory nature of things, they can—and do—easily, quickly, and subtly take over our lives and attitudes. Possessions have a way of "owning" us. They can dictate the use of our time and direct the focus of our lives.

Consider the incredible story of those early Christians! The "things" of this world did not control their attitudes. Even when losing their possessions, they were not robbed of joy. Rather, they "joyfully accepted" the reality of their situations and celebrated because their lives were rooted in God-love and not in things (see Heb. 10:34, NIV).

Reality check: In what ways do material possessions tend to control us?

Don't material possessions have a sneaky way of controlling our priorities, establishing our goals, and dictating the use of our finances and time? We get so wrapped up in things that when we lose them, we lose our joy. We become trapped. If this happens, then our joy is rooted in the wrong reality. This is a choice we make and will find this decision to be an empty cistern.

Review the principle. Check your thermostat of love. What is it set at?

## The Trap Called *Worry*

This is an inner trap, resulting from being anxious about the future. What is the bottom line of worry? That is, why do you worry? What can you do about this life-robbing trap?

In his book *Slaying the Giants in Your Life*, David Jeremiah writes, "We find so many inconsistent, irrational, illogical, ineffective, and irreligious factors when we take a close look at worry. We have as much reason to avoid it as we do some deadly narcotic—that's exactly what it is. But perhaps you've already become dependent upon that drug. Perhaps you need to become free from its tyranny. How can you do it?" (p.62).

Jesus said some significant things about worry. Listen thoughtfully and with confident expectation to what he said about this.

## Matt. 6:24–34.

- Your priorities: Put God and his kingdom first.
- Your daily life: God provides for the birds how much more valuable are you? And will he not provide for you?
- Your security: He cares for the flowers. How much more will he care for you. Your security is in him. What are the necessities in your life? Do you believe he is able to provide! Again, keep the kingdom of God as your first priority.
- Your future: God is in charge of tomorrow and years to come. Relax and enjoy every day.

What conclusions do you have concerning Jesus's teaching about worry? Do you really believe him? Is he trustworthy and capable of doing what he says he will do? How do you think the reality of God's love, which he has put in you by the Holy Spirit, should affect your attitude of worry?

Prayerfully consider a few more verses and set them firmly in your heart and mind.

**1 Pet. 5:7.** *Give all your worries and cares to God, for he cares about what happens to you* (NLT).

**Ps. 55:22.** Give all your worries and cares to God, and he will take care of you. He will *not permit the godly to slip and fall* (NLT).

**Phil. 4:6.** *Do not be anxious about anything.* That includes everything I think.

**Rom. 15:13.** May the God of hope fill you with all joy and peace as you trust in him, so that you may overflow with hope by the power of the Holy Spirit.

The hope, joy, and peace of this verse is the song of a heart that is trusting in God. Living with confident expectation in God's love results in a worry-free heart.

Friends, this is not just theory. It is real. During my pastoral years, we were renting a house on a land contract. The owner moved to another state and was not willing to renew the contract with us. To stay in the house, it was necessary to take over his mortgages—and unfortunately, there were two. This required monthly payments that were beyond our pay scale. One day, a friend took me aside and told me not to worry about financing the house. If I was in need of money, he would provide me with whatever was necessary. It immediately took the pressure off my financial situation. I knew something about this man's integrity. I was fully confident that he could provide whatever was necessary. I knew, too, that he was fully trustworthy, competent, and capable of doing what he said. How much more, then, you can trust in God! He has limitless wealth. He is fully trustworthy. He is totally competent to do what he promises. To trust God without reservations is to know freedom from worry. As I trusted my friend, so you can trust God—or do you prefer to look inward and worry? Worry is a trap! What are you planning to do about it? Must this trap be an ongoing daily experience in your life?

Jesus gave you and me a challenge, a promise, a model and a command. Very carefully and thoughtfully consider what he said. "I have loved you even as the Father has loved me. Remain in my love. When you obey me, you remain in my love, just as I obey my Father and remain in his love. I have told you this so that you will be filled with my joy. Yes, your joy will overflow! I command you to love each other in the same way that I love you" (John 15:9–12).

You may be thinking at this point, "How can I ever live this way? I don't think I can learn to live with such an attitude and behavior. I hardly expect to experience this kind of worry-free, joy-filled living." And you are right. This is not ordinary for any of us. We are ordinary people who have an extraordinary gift. Remember what God has poured into you by the Holy Spirit: his love. We must learn to nurture and draw upon God's gift. Only then can we live as he commands. That is his desire for each of us.

## Yes, You Can!

Think about how you learned to ice skate. Was it not by practice and thereby developing and growing in this skill? Likewise, we can put into practice the "skill" of trusting God and living the way he desires. We *can* grow in trust and experience his joy. He promises it. "So, dear brothers, you have no obligation whatsoever to do what your sinful nature urges you to do. For if you keep on following it, you will perish. But if through the power of the Holy Spirit you turn from it and its evil deeds, you will live (Rom. 8:12–14).

Are you celebrating the joy of the Lord in your life? If you are not celebrating such joy, check your thermostat of love. Where is it set?

# PEACE: A MANIFESTATION OF GOD'S LOVE

Peace is a marvelous extension of God's love that we all desire, yet it is so elusive. We have it, but then it slips from our hearts and minds like water running through our fingers. Something happens, and then it's gone.

Jesus is our source of true peace, not this culture we live in or the standards and promises offered by this world. Jesus said, "I am leaving you with a gift—peace of mind and heart. And the peace I give isn't like the peace the world gives. So don't be troubled or afraid" (John 14:27). And again, "I have told you all this so that you may have peace in me. Here on earth you will have many trials and sorrows. But take heart, because I have overcome the world (John 16:33).

The word *world* describes not the planet, Earth, but rather humanity in its fallenness and rebellion against God (see 1 John 2:15–17; John 17:13–26; Col. 2:20–23).

What a contrast! Doesn't the reality of this world give us much cause to be fearful and troubled? Yet, Jesus tells us not to be troubled and not to be afraid?

This can be true in us because the peace of Jesus:

o Enables composure even in difficult times (John 14:1).
o Is meant to rule in our lives so that we, as God's people, can live in peace (Col. 3:15).
o Is a reality in God's kingdom (Rom. 14:17).

Therefore, to know peace we are to nurture God's gift of his love and practice it daily:

o in our homes.
o in all our relationships, and circumstances.
o with the people with whom we rub shoulders each day.

Jesus gives us a peace we can celebrate even though in this world we will experience trouble and turmoil.

Imagine walking past a house with a yard that is not much more than a collection of junk, and the house itself needs urgent repair. Then one day we begin to see good things happening. New owners have moved in. The yard is cleaned up, the grass has been mowed, and flowers have been planted. The house is painted, the windows repaired. The inside is also renovated and beautifully decorated. So it is with us when Jesus takes up residence in our lives. Changes take place and beautiful things happen. Our lives (i.e., our houses) begins to change in enriching beautiful ways.

It isn't religion that keeps us close to God, but rather our walk in God's love. Out of the love the Holy Spirit has put in us emerges the manifestations of his love in all its beauty and fullness (John 7:39).

It seems, then, that if we are to experience the peace of God, we are to love God with a wholehearted passion and extend this gift to others. The result will be to experience the peace of God. If you are not experiencing peace, check your thermostat of love. Where is it set?

# PATIENCE: A MANIFESTATION OF GOD'S LOVE

Patience or longsuffering: "Longsuffering is that quality or self-restraint in the face of provocation which does not hastily retaliate or promptly punish: it is the opposite of anger and is associated with mercy, and is used of God, Exod. 34:6; Rom. 2:4; 1 Pet. 3:20 (W. E. Vine, *An Expository Dictionary of New Testament Words*, p. 116).

To put this differently, because God's love has been given to us through the Holy Spirit (Rom. 5:5), we have within us the resource to be longsuffering or patient. That means we can endure injuries inflicted upon us by others. We are enabled by God's love to accept irritating or painful situations and to respond with confidence in God's love and faithfulness.

I have a coffee mug at home that has an inscription that I like. It reads, "Grant me patience, Lord ... and please grant it to me now." I like the contradiction of the statement because I think it expresses what most people want: quick answers from God. We usually do not think about the foundation necessary to receive the gift of patience. Often, we mistakenly think it is an extension of God's grace that exists all by itself, unrelated to any other qualities of God. But as we will see, God's love is the necessary source for patience and for all manifestations of his love.

The following is an imaginary story designed to communicate the truths expressed in this book. The scene is of a father and mother visiting with their pastor. They are disturbed by their relationship with their daughter, so they visit their pastor to ask for prayer.

He enquires about their concern. Both confirm that communication with their daughter has seriously deteriorated. They confess frustration that every attempt to communicate with her results in anger—both from their daughter and from each of them.

"Pastor, we are asking you to pray for us. We urgently need patience. We love our daughter and know that we must do something to change the path she is traveling."

The pastor replies, "I have no doubt you have prayed earnestly for patience, and you are here because you have not received an answer. I've got good news for you so that you can rejoice in the patience you are searching for and in restoring communication with your daughter. The Bible tells us the fruit of the Spirit is love. This is an extraordinary love, one unlike any other kind. It is what I call *God-love*. This extraordinary gift has been given to you. It manifests itself in a variety of ways, including in patience. Now, let me ask you a very important question. When you talk with your daughter, do your words and voices communicate God's love to her? Or does your anger reveal your self-centeredness? Those are important questions. You must be honest with yourself.

"It is important to remember how much God loves you. You need to pray for God's love to fill your hearts, minds, and tongues. When God-love is real in you and not just a theological idea, it will be evident in your heart and mind, in your words, and in your tone of voice. In contrast, your anger reveals that you are talking to your daughter from your self-centeredness and not from the love God has poured into you. You are supposed to be an agent of his love. As husband and wife, when you pray with each other, pray for God-love to become real in your hearts and minds and words. Then you will be patient with your daughter.

"Do you see how this is significantly different than just praying for patience? What this means is that you have a unique privilege to be involved in a working fellowship with Jesus your Lord. You and Jesus are laboring together. It's not just you, your patience, and your daughter. Remember, he is Lord—not you. He is the one who will change attitudes and replace anger with patience. He will bless you with other manifestations of love, such as kindness and self-control. It is God's love that brings healing and that will restore relationships between you and your daughter.

"Do you believe God's love can do that? Do you believe Jesus is able do what you cannot do to renew and restore relationships? Believe! Pray wholeheartedly and trust unreservedly for God-love to flow through each of you in your attitudes, words, and tones of voice. Talk to your daughter with such love, and expect good things to happen because God is able and because you are in a working fellowship with him. To put this simply, in a phrase I use to help myself remember, you are in sales (i.e., you love her), but God is in management (i.e., he will change her). Don't ever mix those two up.

"Believing in the Lord means trusting him to work according to his timetable with sovereign power to change both you and your daughter, according to His wisdom and eternal love."

God is able! Believe him with confidence, and trust him with expectation. If you find you still have trouble with anger and impatience, check your love level with the Lord.

What kind of clothes are you wearing? That may seem like a strange question, but it is the key to our daily lives.

Since God chose you to be holy people, whom he loves, you must clothe yourselves with tenderhearted mercy, kindness, humility, gentleness, and patience. You must make allowances for each other's faults and forgive the person who offends you. Remember, the Lord forgave you, so you must forgive others. And the most important piece of clothing you must wear is love (Col. 3:12–14). So, what clothes are you wearing?

The Bible tells us that "love is patient" (1 Cor. 13:4). So, if you are impatient, check your thermostat of love. Are you responding from the gift of God's love or from self-centeredness? This is a good checkpoint from which to grow.

Be encouraged! "For God is working in you, giving you the desire to obey him and the power to do what pleases him" (Phil. 2:13).

# Kindness and Goodness: Two Manifestations of God's Love

God created us. He knows our frail natures, our weaknesses, our self-centeredness, and our daily struggles. He fully understands the evils of this world. Thus, it becomes even more urgent that we extend kindness and goodness into our daily lives. Doing this extends God's love. It puts the gift he has poured into us into practice with others. He instructs and empowers us to be his image bearers (Phil. 2:13) in this world. We are to be light in a world of darkness. This is God's desire for his people. That's you and me. Now, let's look at these two manifestations of God's love. We will come to understand this truth when we practice it. We can live with confident expectation knowing it is the power of God's love that produces kindness and goodness.

These two manifestations of God's love are uniquely

distinctive, and yet, as you will see, they share similarities. For this reason, each will be considered in this lesson.

## Kindness

This refers to the attitude of the heart. It is our inner disposition toward others and toward life situations. Kindness is an attitude of warmth that is compassionately hungry for the well-being of others. In fact, there is never a time when you are responding in God's love that is not rooted in kindness. Kindness is the nature of God and is to be the heart attitude of every follower of Jesus, as noted in Luke 6:35 and Eph. 4:32.

Consider this daily challenge! The Lord's servants must not quarrel but must be kind to everyone. They must be able to teach effectively and be patient with difficult people. Being kind does not mean always having an upbeat personality or being coated with sweetness or niceness. It is not about simply seeking approval. Kindness is about being honest, yet always loving. It is a manifestation of God's love. Our goal is not to change a person; only God has the power to change a person's heart. But you and I are to be faithful, remembering that we are in a working fellowship with Jesus. Our part is to extend his love and trust Jesus to use this bridge for his own purpose and in his time. For us, the pressure is off. Our God-given purpose is to reach out to hurting people and to do so with kindness.

If you discover that kindness is not a quality of caring for others, then you should check your thermostat of God's love. What does it read?

## Goodness

There is a very close relationship between kindness and goodness. Kindness is the condition of the heart that expresses God's love with warmth and genuine care. It is not domineering or arrogant; it is compassionate.

Goodness is not quite the same as kindness, but it has the quality of doing good to others built in. It is a kindly activity that benefits others. It is kindness being expressed in specific helpful ways. It is doing good deeds. It is what we do as a result of the kindness that is in our hearts. As you can see, there is interdependence between these two manifestations of God's love, yet each one is unique.

## Summary:

God planted his love in us through the Holy Spirit (Rom. 5:5). It is God's desire that his people extend this gift to others. This is meant to be an ongoing, daily process of practice and growing. Yesterday's kindness and goodness are not sufficient to meet today's challenges. These are manifestations of God's love that we are called to express to and to experience from others.

Our struggle to live this way is very real. This is a battle that takes place in our inner beings. The battle inside builds up and overflows into words and actions that may or may not express kindness and goodness. "So I advise you to live according to your new life in the Holy Spirit. Then you won't be doing what your sinful nature craves. The old sinful nature loves to do evil, which is just the opposite from what the Holy Spirit wants. And the Spirit gives us desires that are opposite from what the sinful nature desires. These two forces are constantly fighting each other, and your choices are never free from this conflict" (Gal. 5:16–17).

These are qualities worth living for and striving to demonstrate in our daily lives. What a high goal God puts before us! He desires for his people to nurture and develop kindness and express it in good deeds in our homes, churches, workplaces, communities, and in all our relationships and situations.

So, then, it is necessary to nurture these manifestations of God's love daily through studying his word, being faithful in prayer, and through ongoing practice. Then you will grow in experiencing and expressing God-love. It's a life-long journey. Rejoice in your progress, but don't expect perfection. That will not happen until glory. Remember: during your journey, check the thermostat of love to read what it says about your love level. And rejoice because you are growing in your fellowship with Jesus.

# FAITHFULNESS:
# A MANIFESTATION
# OF GOD'S LOVE

Location! Location! Location! If you are planning to start a business, realtors will tell you that "location, location, location" is the key. The reasons for this are obvious. At the time of this writing, we are living near a shopping mall that is having trouble keeping businesses. Every time we walk by there, it is obvious that the traffic of customers is very low. We wonder how the mall can remain open. Many businesses have moved out for lack of customers. Location, location, location is the first principle.

The first principle in interpreting scripture is context, context, and context! What, then, does this mean in terms of faithfulness? How are we to understand this in light of the present context? As with all the manifestations, the key is God-love.

It was but a few days before Jesus entered Jerusalem to

begin his journey to Calvary. Now, in these last hours with his disciples, Jesus was bringing his earthly ministry to its conclusion. In these crucial, final moments together, Jesus spoke to his disciples, commanding them not just to teach the truth, but also to live it in a radical new way. Can you imagine spending three years with Jesus, seeing his miracles, hearing his wisdom, and being amazed in the journey with him? Then, suddenly, Jesus challenges them—and us—with a summary of what it means to be one of his followers, not just in name, but in the reality of everyday living. "A new commandment I give you." This is not a suggestion; it is an order from the highest authority. It is not an option he gave, but rather authoritative marching orders. He doesn't leave us wondering what that means. He tells us to "love one another as I have loved you." He is our example to follow. It is not a matter of guessing, but rather, it is about doing what he taught and demonstrated. Wow! He goes on to explain further: This love, is how you will prove to the world that you are my disciples. This love, which is grace, puts how Jesus lived and what he taught, which is truth, into practice.

Faithfulness is how we demonstrate God's love. It is easily understood. There is no mysterious or hidden meaning connected with it; it is the obvious meaning of being trustworthy and loyal. That is easily understood, but it's not so easily put into practice. We have a problem, a serious problem: we are all broken, imperfect, sinful people.

Faithfulness is an indispensable part of God's love. Therefore, it is essential for us to be faithful. But, faithful in what sense? Basically, it is the same as in all the other manifestations of God's love: we are to be faithful in knowing and extending God's love into any situation. If you are not living in God's love, what do you think the result will be? For instance, you are having a discussion with a friend. But the discussion begins to get heated, which has a way of short-circuiting your ability to remain focused in God's love and instead become agitated in self-centeredness. Your ego is taking over, and the desire to be right takes control. What has happened to kindness, goodness, gentleness, and patience? If you paused to check your thermostat of God's love, you would probably find it reading near zero.

Here's another illustration: I was sitting in my living room one day when I noticed a beautiful rainbow of colors on the far wall. *Where did that come from?* I wondered. Looking around, I noticed that light came through our windows and passed through a prism of glass on our bookcase. This prism took what was invisible and projected the rainbow of colors onto the far wall. That's what happens when we are "prisms" of God's love. His invisible love projects understanding, peace, joy, patience, kindness, and all the other manifestations of his love.

The key is to have faithfulness in God's love. Again, check your thermostat of God's love. What does it read? If the conversation with your friend went out of control because of your emotions and ego, the thermostat is probably low. But don't despair; God knows we are weak and in need of his help. Forgive and be renewed in his goodness. Understand every experience as an important learning occasion and grow from it. Rejoice in progress. Perfection will not be experienced until your future glory.

# GENTLENESS: A MANIFESTATION OF GOD'S LOVE

Gentleness is a tangible extension of God-love. Hence, it is important to have a clear understanding of this manifestation love. It is a difficult word to translate into English because it has no precise equivalent. The commonly used words *meekness*, *mildness*, and *gentleness* do not quite capture the full meaning of the Greek word *prautes*. These English words suggest weakness, lacking courage, without firm resolution, and timidity. Such notions have no part in *prautes*. This word describes a person's mind and heart, which know God's grace and *intentionally* extend that grace into real-life situations. Such behavior is not rooted in weakness, does not lack in courage, and is not timid. Rather, *prautes* is the result of a *deliberate* decision that is rooted in power and uncommon strength. Such a quality of life does not come from a position of feeble impotence, but rather from a tremendous inner strength that is rooted in the Holy Spirit.

We are talking here about extending God's love into life situations that can be easy or difficult, joyful or painful, encouraging or discouraging, life-enriching or life-robbing. However, in every situation, the grace of God—and so the love of God—should be extended. This is no easy task. "Even a cursory glance at the content of God's love discloses that here we are face to face with a powerful, potent life principle. We are dealing with a divine dimension of living, a radical lifestyle. God grant that within us there might be generated an enormous, overwhelming, irresistible desire to become like him who is *love* … to have reproduced in us the fruit of His life" (Phillip Keller, *A Gardner Looks at the Fruits of the Spirit*, 486–87).

People are fragile. Have you experienced that? I can't remember how many times I have been hurt by others who were insensitive or arrogant or absolute or overzealous or overbearing in their opinions. Have you met such people— they who somehow know exactly what you must do and be. Gentleness is not a quality of their aromas. How did you respond to encounters with such people? Even worse than that, each of us needs to ask ourselves how we have offended others because of our own arrogance, self-centered insensitivities, and failures to be thoughtful or gentle.

God's expectation for us is clear. He calls us to:

A preferred relationship: He tells how he expects his followers to live in a challenging, sinful world. The Christian life is not just about theology or religious talk. It is about living as God desires and as he has equipped us. That means living with a quiet confident God-Love with gentleness (1 Cor. 4:21).

A caring spirit: Gentleness is to be the underlying spirit with which we reach out to hurting people who have made wrong decisions in their lives, who have become trapped in sinful behaviors. They need someone to come alongside them with gentleness and encouragement (Gal. 6:1). This is God's way.

A worthy life: We are to be humble and gentle with each other, making allowance for faults in our fallen humanity. We have been called by God to extend his love. This is the power that changes people's hearts. None of us is perfect, so don't expect perfection in others. Let God's love be your motivating spirit (Eph. 4:1–3).

A visible quality: "Rejoice in the Lord always. I will say it again: Rejoice. Let your gentleness be evident to all" (Phil. 4:4–5, NIV).

Again, have you checked your thermostat of love lately? Remember, God-love is the key, and you are in a significant working fellowship with Jesus. Your job is to extend his love, which, in this case, is gentleness.

# SELF-CONTROL: A MANIFESTATION OF THE LOVE OF GOD

Self-control: We have a significant role in this discipline, but don't become confused as to what that role is. We who are followers of Jesus have an extraordinary reason to practice self-control. In fact, we have more motivation than anyone else to nurture and grow in practicing this quality of God's love in our daily lives. You and I are not called to change other people's hearts, mind, or lives. We are called to be channels of grace. Jesus planted his love in us through the Holy Spirit. Now he expects us to draw upon that gift and pass it on to others. But it is precisely at this point that we must understand our roles: to extend his love to others. That is our God-given task. It is in this manifestation of his love that Jesus—not you or I—changes people's minds and hearts and lives. Do not get those two mixed up.

To illustrate this point, let's say that we are in sales,

extending his love, and he is management, changing hearts and lives. I have shared this truth with numerous people, and a comment I often receive is that it gives wonderful freedom, hope, and confidence. We can rejoice because we have faithfully done what Jesus desires of us, and we can trust him to change people according to his purpose, plan, and time. Ask yourself this question: Do you really trust Jesus, who loves you and who has poured his love into you, that he will do what he says? What does it mean to have a working fellowship with Jesus? This is the vital question. The answer gives real hope and strength to practice self-control. Alternately, is this idea of a working fellowship with Jesus only theoretical in your life? Are you like Adam and Eve, who believed that God's word was not sufficient and, like them, think you have to add your own wisdom and strength to be effective?

An elder friend who deeply loved the Lord and was committed to sharing God's love whenever he could. However, he shared with me how frustrated he was that no one seemed to respond in faith by believing and accepting Jesus as their savior. We talked, and I explained that he could not do the job of Jesus. Only Jesus can change a person heart and life. Instead of trying to do Jesus's job, he needed to rejoice that he was doing what Jesus desired of him—namely, sharing the love of God with others. Then he could trust Jesus to do his part.

And now, friends, I ask you to reread the words of Jesus carefully as he describes what it means to have a working fellowship with him. See the first pages of this text for more information.

As with all the other manifestations of God's love, if you are struggling with self-control—which is a normal human dilemma—check your thermostat of love.

Let the words of this old hymn be part of your daily prayer!

"May the mind of Christ my Savior *live* in me from day to day, *by his love and pow'r, controlling all I do and say.*"

*The fruit of the Spirit is love, God-love.*

*It is the mind of God.*

*It is the ethic of the entire Bible,*

*and*

*It is God's desire for all his people.*

# THINK ABOUT IT:
# YOUR PERSONAL
# APPLICATION

Because he has poured his love into us by the Holy Spirit, he expects us to extend this gift to others with conviction and confidence that, through the Holy Spirit, we are equipped for the opportunities and challenges he puts into our paths. This means living with confident expectation and trusting him with the results.

John 7:38 (NIV) says, "Whoever believes in me, as the scripture has said, streams of living water will flow from within him." This living water includes the fruit of the Spirit—namely, love expressing itself in joy, peace, patience, kindness, goodness, faithfulness, gentleness, and self-control.

The following is a personal exercise to encourage you to evaluate yourself, extend the love of God in specific ways, and encourage growth in the daily practice of God-love. It is not enough simply to know God's love. It has been given to be put into practice. Change and growth only become real in the specifics of life.

This personal worksheet will make an excellent prayer guide, so be honest. This is between you and the Lord.

Brief comments are given before each section for the purpose of stimulating your thinking process. Consider each of the following manifestations of God's love. Write down your responses to the questions or statements. Be honest because this can be a very valuable tool to review your progress—or lack thereof.

For easy reference, page numbers refer to this manual.

## Page 1: **A Working Fellowship with Jesus, Your Lord.**

Each word of this title is important. Consider the following statements. These are essential to understand the relevance of this study.

*Working.* What does this say to you?

*Fellowship.* What does this tell you about your relationship with Jesus and others?

Consider1 John 1:3a–3b, 1:6, and 1:7. Notice the richness of fellowship with each other and with God.

*Jesus, Your Lord.* Is it possible to have Jesus as your savior and not as your Lord? Discuss how this relates to your daily living.

<u>Page 4</u>: **The Important Question.**

Discuss the significance of Paul saying, "the *fruit* of the Spirit is …" and not "the *fruits* of the Spirit are …"

## Page 5: God's Love Is the Key to Understanding.

Discuss 1 Cor. 13:1–7. What is the love that Paul is talking about? Why do you think he considers this so crucial?

"God's love does not seek to manipulate. It is not done for self-gratification. It does not seek to control. So, be alert in practicing God's love that it does not become a tool for manipulation, legalism, or self-aggrandizement" (page 6 in this text). Do you agree with this statement? Why or why not?

In light of the above statements, how is God's love evident in your life?

<u>Page 7:</u> **Joy: A Manifestation of God's Love.**

What do you think of Phillip Keller's distinction between happiness and joy?

*Carlton Baker*

What happens to *joy* when you become critical of others, angry, or negative?

Several "traps" that rob you of joy are circumstances, people, things, and worry. How would you rate yourself in each one? How do they rob you of joy? Why?

Consider *worry*, as noted in Matt. 6:24–32. How can these words of Jesus help you to deal with this major thief of your joy?

<u>Page 13:</u> **Peace: A Manifestation of God's Love.**

How would you define peace?

What situations or relationships in your life have resulted in the loss of peace?

Can you describe how or why this happened?

Jesus said, "I have told you all this so that you may peace in me." How do you think this statement would help you to celebrate the peace that Jesus gives?

In the same breath, Jesus said, "Here on earth you will have many trials and sorrows. But take heart, I have overcome the world" (John 16:33b). How do you harmonize these two statements? That is, how can you have peace in the midst of such turmoil?

What a contrast! Doesn't the reality of this world give us much cause to be fearful and troubled? Jesus tell us not be troubled and not to be afraid. How can this be?

Note: The word *world* describes not planet Earth, but rather humanity in its fallenness and rebellion against God (see 1 John 2:15–17; John 17:13–26; and Col. 2:22–23).

<u>Page 14:</u> **Patience: A Manifestation of God's Love.**

Patience is trusting God with His solutions. He knows the brokenness of all people. Patience does not seek to manipulate or control people or circumstances. God-love produces patience.

Do you agree with this statement? What are your reasons for agreeing or disagreeing?

How is your patience evident to others?

*Carlton Baker*

How are you celebrating patience in your inner self?

What situations or relationships have resulted in the loss of your patience? Why or how do you think this happened?

What is your reaction to the advice the pastor gave the husband and wife about how to proceed with their daughter?

What specific steps can you take to practice patience in your own life?

## Pages 16 and 17: **Kindness and Goodness: Two Manifestations of God's Love.**

These two manifestations of God's love are distinctive, yet as you will see, they share similarities.

*Kindness* is the attitude of the heart. It is an inner attitude of warmth that is compassionately hungry for the well-being of others.

*Carlton Baker*

How do others see the evidence of kindness in your heart?

None of us is perfect, so kindness is not always a reality in our lives. Why is this so? What situations or relationships have dampened your kindness toward others?

When kindness is lacking, how do you relate to others, if at all?

<u>Page 17</u>: *Goodness* is kindness in action. It is the overflowing of a heart that knows God's goodness. It is this heart condition that is expressed in specific ways.

*Carlton Baker*

What are some ways that you express goodness?

None of us is perfect. What situations or relationships rob you from extending goodness?

*Carlton Baker*

Since this is an extension of God's love, how can you prepare yourself to share his goodness?

<u>Page 19</u>: **Faithfulness Is a Manifestation of God's Love.**

Faithfulness means not giving up. It means being loyal and trustworthy. The other person is so important that faithfulness continues to extend the gift of love he has planted in us. God's love results in faithfulness.

*Carlton Baker*

How is this gift of faithfulness evident in your life?

We are all broken, hurting people. Sometimes, in the course of our daily lives, we are like porcupines backing into each other.

*Carlton Baker*

How can you specifically extend love in such a situation?

<u>Page 20:</u> **Gentleness Is a Manifestation of God's Love**.

It knows people are fragile. Gentleness relates to others with compassion, sensitivity, and caring. This means we will not respond in revenge or retribution, regardless of what the other person has said or done.

Biblically speaking, gentleness does not have the ordinary meaning that is often attributed to it. See page 21 of this text for the meaning of the Greek word *prautes*, which is often translated as *goodness*. I think you will be surprised.

With this understanding of gentleness, how do you think it will affect your practice?

<u>Page22:</u> **Self-Control Is a Manifestation of God's Love.**

We have a significant role in this discipline. We who are followers of Jesus have an extraordinary reason to practice self-control. In responding to people, we are to restrain our passions, personal desires, and self-centered goals. Instead, we are to truly listen, understand, and rationally respond— always with the love that God has planted in our heart.

In light of the above statement how well are you doing in self-control?

Share what happened when you lost control and also what happened when God's love controlled you.

None of us is perfect, so in honesty, what causes you to lose self-control?

Don't think you are alone. This is a typical human problem. What plans or strategies do you have to prepare yourself for to deal with this problem?

As with all the manifestations of the Spirit, how has God's love been involved in your self-control?

# Final Thoughts

To pursue this further in your own life, think about what controls you in any given situation. Is it the love of God being extended into the situation, or is it self-centeredness or self-gratification? Is there an attitude or behavior that needs to be given to God and for which you should ask for forgiveness? If so, pray for God's love to control your attitudes and actions. In so living, you will experience the manifestations of the fruit of the Spirit when controlled by the love of God (2 Cor. 5:14–15).

Since we live by the Spirit, let us
keep in step with the Spirit.

—Gal. 5:25 (NIV)

Printed in the United States
By Bookmasters